I0087357

How To Press Forward & Shift To A Higher Level

Living a Vocal, Valued and Victorious Life (Vol. 2)

JO ANNE MEEKINS

Inspired 4 U

Publications

Copyright © 2014 Jo Anne Meekins.

Scriptures references from the Holy Bible.

Published by Inspired 4 U Publications,
an imprint of Inspired 4 U Ministries, LLC.

September 2014

ISBN-13: 978-0692274958
ISBN-10: 0692274952

DEDICATION

This book is dedicated to fellow poet and author Malik "Word Bird" Canty and my church family at Apostolic Temple of Jesus Christ (AToJC). Their hands-on acts of love, friendship, encouragement, and support helped me to press forward and shift to a higher level through an extremely challenging time of hardship and family tragedy.

Because of you, I did not drown in the a sea of overwhelm while dealing with mom's sudden health crises. Instead, I pressed forward and completed four books; published a client's book (Tears For My Ancestors by Malik Canty); participated as a speaker in the 4 Divas For Divas World Conference; and as a client in two coaching programs (Speaking2Inspire with Coach Sheya Chisenga and the 30-Day List Building Challenge with Coach Keisha "Rocks" Lewis).

Your continued support is valued and sincerely appreciated. I love you all dearly.

Special shout out to AToJC Pastor Marcus McKnight, The Mothers Board, The Board of Trustees, The Missionary Board, The Women's Choir, and Sis. Cauline Williams, who has been buying multiple copies of "How To Uncover, Heal & Release Painful Life Experiences: Living a Vocal, Valued and Victorious Life (Vol. 1)" as a gift for anyone God puts on her heart to share them with!

Glory be to God!

CONTENTS

ACKNOWLEDGMENTS

First and foremost, I honor and thank God
for His inspired words that flow through me limitlessly.

Secondly, it is my pleasure to acknowledge Sales Expert Che Brown, Marketing Guru Trevor Otts, and Media Queen Dr. Letitia Wright. They are the producers and speaker coordinator of the 4 Divas For Divas World Conference. It is because of my participation in this event that the Living a Vocal, Valued and Victorious Life three-volume series was birthed.

As one of the speakers for the 4 Divas For Divas event, I was challenged to come up with a product offering to share during my presentation. In my brainstorming and preparation, I realized that I had enough written material to categorize into three books that signified my life experience and reflected my core beliefs and message to the world. The results are:

1. How To Uncover, Release & Heal Painful Life Experiences
2. How to Press Forward & Shift to a Higher Level
3. How To Know God Better & Love Yourself More

I am grateful to God and these individuals, who have been instrumental in my shift to a higher level as I press forward toward the prize of my high calling.

NOTE: The 4 Divas For Divas World Conference airs on September 13, 2014 and features sensational women speakers with unique perspectives on personal and professional development packed into one full day of invaluable information, power networking with other divas, and life-changing inspiration.

Access to the speakers' presentations will be made available after the event for anyone interested in reviewing the video replays and taking notes at their leisure.

Contact me at JoAnneMeekins@inspired4uministries.com for information regarding the Speakers' library of experiences and expertise that will provide you with the tools you need to be a Dynamic Diva, both personally and professionally.

"*I press toward the goal for the prize of the upward call of God in Christ Jesus.*"
(Philippians 3:14)

HOW TO TURN TOWARD YOUR DESTINY

Like Jonah did before his encounter with the big fish, are you going in the opposite direction of where God has called you to go? Or, has a fearful spirit hindered you from stepping into a higher level of leadership or path of purpose? If so, in order for you to turn toward your destiny, you must change direction at some point in time.

When God is dealing with you, it's time to settle the internal conflict and make decisions. And it has to be a 100% commitment because 99½ won't do! That ½ percent of inner resistance is an indication of double-mindedness that can block your progress.

(James 1:5-8) *"If any of you lacks wisdom, you should ask God, who gives generously to all without finding fault, and it will be given to you. ⁶But when you ask, you must believe and not doubt, because the one who doubts is like a wave of the sea, blown and tossed by the wind. ⁷That person should not expect to receive anything from the Lord. ⁸Such a person is double-minded and unstable in all they do."*

Therefore, purpose in your heart and mind to surrender all to Jesus, realizing that in order to overcome, you have to do that which you fear.

For those of you who can relate, are facing challenges, or are at a fork in your journey, I offer the following first hand insights to turning point opportunities:

1. **Acknowledge** – Acknowledge the fears and the fact that you are not on your truest path.

2. **Determine** – Decide to make different choices, to set goals, and take steps in the right direction in spite of the fear.

3. **Act** – Respond to the decision with a tangible action. Do something that has been pressing on you and you know to be right, but you have avoided doing it.

4. **Learn** – Recognize what transpired through your experience and document what it was, how you handled it, and what lessons you learned.

5. **Remember** – Remember the experience as a positive testimony to review or share during a time when you may need to encourage yourself or someone else.

There is no way to successfully escape the plan and purpose that God has ordained for your life. To go in the opposite direction will only cause painful consequences for you and others around you. Decide to surrender to the process, face your fears, and turn toward your destiny.

HOW TO SHIFT FROM WHERE YOU ARE TO WHERE YOU DESIRE TO BE

The following steps are a practical application to moving forward in your life, from a seemingly unpleasant and uncomfortable place of waiting into a desired place of the heart:

1. **Engage in spiritual practices** – Spiritual practices can help you identify where you are and what is going on from the inside out. What you see on the outside in your life is a direct reflection of what you are thinking and feeling about yourself and your experiences. Practices such as:

- Journaling – Writing about your thoughts and feelings, present and past

- Prayer and Meditation – Seeking God's direction, listening for His instruction and being obedient to what you hear

- Love, Forgiveness, and Gratitude – Walking in the foundation of the Christian commitment and the keys to victorious living

Operating in these principles daily will help you identify

where you are and clearly see what you authentically desire to do.

2. **Seek out and maintain a connection to a spiritual support base** – Churches, prayer line teleconferences, and coaching relationships are just a few spiritual communities that can help you hold on to your dreams, regardless of what the circumstances look or feel like. These relationships can hold you accountable, speak life to your soul, and cover you with loving kindness and the assurance that you are not alone.

3. **Be expectant and faith-filled** – Speak and write what you truly desire to experience and possess in life. Think about it and feel with certainty that it will happen without a doubt. Listen to what your body is signaling to you and identify the following:

- Knowing that it is a sure thing, how do you feel?

- How is your body expressing that feeling?

- What emotions are present for you in the moment of feeling your desire become a reality?

Hold on to those good feelings with expectancy and recapture them whenever you need to overcome negative emotions and experience a happy place of joy and fulfillment.

4. **Decide the shift has taken place** – Make up in your mind that you are already in a new season and day of power and prosperity, killing off all other options. Know that you co-create your life with divine guidance and personal fortitude; and that you create the exact amount of your financial success. Determine to do whatever it takes, in accordance to God's will, to experience the life you desire.

5. **Take action** – Do things differently to get different results. Insanity is defined as repeatedly doing the same thing the same way, expecting different results. Take a tangible step

in the direction of your desires, goals, or dreams. But:

> ✓ First, *ask* God what actions will propel you into a breakthrough experience
>
> ✓ Second, *allow* Him to provide the opportunities, sources, and way to where you desire to be

Seeking God first will allow you to take action steps doing what you love and live the abundant life He intentionally planned and purposed, customized just for you.

HOW TO LIVE YOUR DREAM NOW

Resurrection Is A Lifestyle - LIVE IT!

Are you suffering from the heart sickness of a dream deferred? If so, the resurrection of your hope is at hand. Resurrection is not limited to the Easter season; it can be an everyday experience as in the motto coined by my former Brooklyn church St. Paul Community Baptist Church: "Resurrection is a Lifestyle – LIVE IT!"

Each time you endure and persevere through another year, you are an overcomer, who has been given an opportunity to live another day and contribute to making a difference with your life. With each new day, you have a chance to begin again, continue on, tap into your creative force, and realize your divine self.

If your dreams have been held captive by fears and insecurities too long, apply the following principles for your liberation and success. Now is the time and this is the season to resurrect your dreams and make them live!

EMBRACE WHAT YOU KNOW

• **Know And Embrace Yourself**. Know that you have been born with at least one gift, talent, or ability; and you are blessed with unlimited potential. Step into your future with hope for the peace, prosperity, and security that is yours. If you can believe and look for it wholeheartedly, you will find it. Everything you need to make your dream a reality is already within you. Know and embrace yourself.

(Psalm 139:13-16) *Oh yes, you shaped me first inside, then out; you formed me in my mother's womb. I thank you, High God — you're breathtaking! Body and soul, I am marvelously made! I worship in adoration — what a creation! You know me inside and out, you know every bone in my body; You know exactly how I was made, bit by bit, how I was sculpted from nothing into something. Like an open book, you watched me grow from conception to birth; all the stages of my life were spread out before you, the days of my life all prepared before I'd even lived one day.*

(Ephesians 4:7-13) *"But that doesn't mean you should all look and speak and act the same. Out of the generosity of Christ, each of us is given his own gift. The text for this is,*

> *He climbed the high mountain,*
> *He captured the enemy and seized the booty,*
> *He handed it all out in gifts to the people.*

Is it not true that the One who climbed up also climbed down, down to the valley of earth? And the One who climbed down is the One who climbed back up, up to highest heaven. He handed out gifts above and below, filled heaven with his gifts, filled earth with his gifts. He handed out gifts of apostle, prophet, evangelist, and pastor-teacher to train Christ's followers in skilled servant work, working within Christ's body, the church, until we're all moving rhythmically and easily with each other, efficient and graceful in response to God's Son, fully mature adults, fully developed within and without, fully alive like Christ."

• **Know And Embrace Your Dream**. When you have a constant and strong desire or interest that has been rooted in your heart and thoughts, embrace it. If it has followed you into each New Year, acknowledge it as your dream, your heart's desire, and determine to pursue it to see what the end is going to be. Put forth 100% effort. In doing so, you will extinguish any regrets of never trying or ever knowing if your dream could be realized.

(Jeremiah 29:11) *"For I know the plans I have for you," declares the Lord, "plans to prosper you and not to harm you, plans to give you hope and a future."*

(Psalm 37:4-5) *"Delight yourself also in the Lord, and He will give you the desires and secret petitions of your heart. Commit your way to the Lord [roll and repose each care of your load on Him]; trust (lean on, rely on, and be confident) also in Him and He will bring it to pass."*

Your dreams and your gifts are deposited in you by God to do a work and be a blessing to others. People are waiting for you. Know and embrace your dream.

• **Know What You Have To Work With**. The wisdom that you need is available. Use what you have, learn what to do, and then do what you know.

✓ Tap into your inner strength and sound mind

✓ Utilize the power and authority you possess

✓ Accept God's unconditional love and hold Him accountable to His faithful promises

✓ Take advantage of the diverse and abundant resources that will be more readily available than ever before

Your thoughts will become clearer and your direction ordered with each step you take toward your plan.

(Proverb 16:3) *"Commit to the Lord whatever you do, and he will establish your plans."*

(Proverbs 3:5-6) *"Lean on, trust in, and be confident in the Lord with all your heart and mind and do not rely on your own insight or understanding. In all your ways know, recognize, and acknowledge Him, and He will direct and make straight and plain your paths."*

Turn within, tap into your inner power, seek and listen to God's direction. Know what you have to work with.

BE POSITIVE AND FAITH-FILLED

• **Counter The Negative With The Positive**. Do not accept a person's put downs or ridicules of you or your dream, even if they are only "joking." Negative words that are planted in our minds have a tendency to sprout up like weeds, choking our creativity with self-doubt and fear.

> ✓ Feed your mind with good things to inspire, enhance, and facilitate growth

> ✓ Do not share your dream with everyone, only share with people you know will genuinely support and encourage you

(2 Corinthians 10:4-5) *"The weapons we fight with are not the weapons of the world. On the contrary, they have divine power to demolish strongholds. We demolish arguments and every pretension that sets itself up against the knowledge of God, and we take captive every thought to make it obedient to Christ."*

Verbally confront people immediately when they make negative or untrue statements to you; state that you do not receive that remark, it is not true, and no longer acceptable. Then make a statement that is true and positive about you or your dream. Counter the negative with the positive.

• **Affirm Yourself Daily**. Practice speaking positive "I" statements that will build up your self-esteem and encourage you to keep striving until you accomplish your goal:

- ✓ I can do it
- ✓ I and my service(s) are needed
- ✓ I am gifted, unique, and special

Call yourself by whatever profession you have chosen:

- ✓ I am an Faith-Based Speaker,
- ✓ I am a Christian Writer
- ✓ I am a Inspirational Publisher and Book Coach
- ✓ I am an Encourager

The more you speak it, the more you will think it. Then, it will begin to take root in your mind, grow in your heart, and blossom into a visualization that you can confidently feel and believe, as it becomes who you are.

(Proverbs 18:20-21) *"Make your words good— you will be glad you did. Words can bring death or life! Talk too much, and you will eat everything you say."*

(Philippians 4:8-9) *"Summing it all up, friends, I'd say you'll do best by filling your minds and meditating on things true, noble, reputable, authentic, compelling, gracious— the best, not the worst; the beautiful, not the ugly; things to praise, not things to curse. Put into practice what you learned from me, what you heard and saw and realized. Do that, and God, who makes everything work together, will work you into his most excellent harmonies."*

You are what you think. Think good thoughts and affirm yourself daily.

• **Do It In The Face Of Fear**. Face your fears and do it anyway, task by task, and day by day. Work your plan, believe in yourself, your dream, the power within you, and expect to see and receive ripe fruit from your labor. Make positive "I" statements out of all the principles and speak them daily:

✓ I will do everything in my power to make my dream a reality

✓ I have a divine purpose and I will work my plan until it is fulfilled

✓ All that I need is readily available within me and within my grasp

✓ I will achieve my greatness; No one nor no-thing can stop or hinder me

✓ I am anointed and appointed to succeed in my creative ministry

✓ I will overcome my fears with each victorious step of faith forward

(Philippians 4:13) *"I have strength for all things in Christ who empowers me [I am ready for anything and equal to anything through Him who infuses inner strength into me; I am self-sufficient in Christ's sufficiency]."*

(2 Timothy 1:7) *"For God did not give us a spirit of timidity (of cowardice, of craven and cringing and fawning fear), but [He has given us a spirit] of power and of love and of a calm and well-balanced mind and discipline and self-control."*

Fear is not of God. Walk in faith and Do it in the face of fear!

I believe that living your dream is relative to one's personal thoughts and actions:

a) Some people harbor doomsday thoughts and give up before they begin. They expect the worse because they have already created their end.

b) Others think it is life as usual, taking it for granted. They exist one day to the next, not taking any risks, until their time is up.

c) Then there are those of us, who choose to believe that the opportunity of a lifetime is at hand to fulfill our divine destinies.

Now is the time and season when the shift has occurred, the field is wide open and the prospects are great for resurrecting your dreams, making them a reality, and living them abundantly. How?

- ✓ Know and embrace yourself and your dream
- ✓ Know what you have to work with
- ✓ Counter the negative with the positive
- ✓ Affirm yourself daily
- ✓ Do it in the face of fear

HOW TO BE PREPARED FOR
UNEXPECTED OPPORTUNITIES

Do you dread the thought of being put on the spot without notice? Have you ever experienced being tongue tied or at a total loss for words in unexpected situations? Have you ever thought of all the things you could have or would have said AFTER an opportunity passed or felt that what you did say probably sounded stupid or scattered to the listener? If so, I offer some suggestions on how to be ready for the unexpected.

First, let me confess that I have not been at my best when placed in unfamiliar, on the spot situations that require me to speak, especially about myself. And on at least two occasions, I experienced the 20-20 hindsight of what I should have said or did, as well as felt that what I did say was all over the place. Which is why after the last experience, I made a decision to define and practice my "30-Second Elevator Speech." The 30-Second Elevator Speech is verbally selling yourself, products, and services in 30 seconds, which is the time it takes to seize a networking opportunity in an elevator with the person getting off on the next floor. This is a tweet example (140 characters)– "I am Jo Anne Meekins, owner of

Inspired 4 U Ministries. I empower women to live vocal, valued and victorious lives and help writers publish."

Now for my preparing for the unexpected suggestions:

1. **Expect the unexpected**! If you have an idea of what you want to do, or you are working towards doing it, or you are already doing it, examine and be clear about your motives (the why behind the what). When your *What* and *Why* are in place, believe and expect that your *How* will show up because ready or not, it will!

2. **View the unexpected encounters and occurrences as opportunities**. Everything that transpires in our lives, whether perceived as good or bad, is an opportunity to learn and grow in various ways, such as in character, endurance, and skill. They are opportunities that can shift you to new levels.

3. **Prepare for opportunity**. Use your senses to solidify what you truly desire, so that you can attract opportunities that align with it.

> ✓ Write down what you desire to experience, expressing all five senses (describe what it looks, sounds, feels, tastes, and smells like)
>
> ✓ Visualize it and make it live. See in detail what you want it to look like at different phases – today, next year, five years from now
>
> ✓ Expect that the opportunities will present themselves and be prepared when they do

A PERSONAL ACTION STEP

After my experience of feeling unprepared at the 2009 Harlem Book Fair, I set an intention to be ready for the next opportunity that I knew would eventually come. I watched a video interview that led me to register for Maria Andros' 10-week Social Media Traffic Blueprint program (SMTB) that teaches how to build a business foundation through video and social media. This represented another example of when you know the why and what, the how will show up. I still have a lot to learn, but a whole new venue that I never considered opened up for me and stimulated new creativity and excitement around the possibilities. This was especially so since I did not consider myself the book signing, street fair vendor, aggressive type and had been seeking to enhance my online presence and learn more about internet marketing.

On the Monday after I became a member of SMTB, another unexpected opportunity presented itself when I dialed into Boost In Your Bathrobe, the 6:00 weekday morning inspiration conference call facilitated by Rev. Valerie Love. Unbeknown to me at the time, Rev. Val had scheduled a guest speaker, who shared my first name, on the call that day. Now, I was at a place in life where I had embraced God's call and strove to walk in it daily; and although I'm not a licensed minister, I was taught and consider all of God's professing people ministers in some form or fashion. So along with the fact that I had been a guest on the call twice before, when Rev. Valerie asked was Min. Jo Anne on the call and no one else responded, I uttered a slow hesitant "Ye-e-e-s." At which point, Rev. Val stated that she was referring to Min. Jo Ann Lee, but since I had spoken up and answered the call it must be for a reason; and then, she told me to share with the group whatever was on my heart.

Even though I wasn't prepared or expecting to share, I knew that God has proven faithful and always shows up. It was not an option for me to not share or speak up and acknowledge that a Min. Jo Anne was indeed on the call. Therefore, I began to share the following from my experience and what was present with me at the time:

1. **Have No Fear Nor Doubt** – Be fully persuaded and confident that God will perform His good work through you if you just make yourself available. Fear is not of God!

(Phil 1:6) *"Being confident of this, that he who began a good work in you will carry it on to completion until the day of Christ Jesus."*

(2 Tim 1:7) *"For God has not given us a spirit of fear, but of power and of love and of a sound mind."*

2. **Say Yes** – Be prepared for any and all opportunities in and out of season, knowing it is not about you. It is God who does the work and works out His will for your life.

(2 Tim 4:2) *"Preach the Word; be prepared in season and out of season; correct, rebuke and encourage— with great patience and careful instruction."*

(Phil 2:13) *"For it is God who works in you to will and to act according to his good purpose."*

3. **Trust God** – Believe that He who promised is faithful to do it. The more He increases in you, the less room there is for fear or doubt. Believe what He says in His word and hold Him accountable to perform it.

(Hebrews 10:23) *"Let us hold fast the confession of our hope without wavering, for He who promised is faithful."*

MIND ISSUES

After I shared those three points, Min. Val asked me to speak to those of us dealing with mind issues. My response was, "Take every thought captive." Anything that is not of God and no longer serves you, nor helps you to function or reach your destination and achieve your goals need to be countered with positive affirmations and the word of God. It takes making a conscious choice daily to focus on the positive and not entertain the negative.

(2 Corinthians 10:4-5) *"The weapons we use in our fight are not the world's weapons but God's powerful weapons, which we use to destroy strongholds. We destroy false arguments; we pull down every proud obstacle that is raised against the knowledge of God; we take every thought captive and make it obey Christ."*

(Phil 4: 8-9) *"Finally, brothers, whatever is true, whatever is noble, whatever is right, whatever is pure, whatever is lovely, whatever is admirable —if anything is excellent or praiseworthy— think about such things. Whatever you have learned or received or heard from me, or seen in me— put it into practice. And the God of peace will be with you."*

In hindsight and partially due to the limited time I had to share and the unexpected opportunity, I added the following thoughts:

EMOTIONAL ISSUES

1. **Praise God** – Sing, dance, pray, and read yourself happy. Do whatever it takes to shift your energy, mindset, attitude, and feelings that are hindering you. Resist the enemy (inner-me) and he has to flee. Cancel the pity party. Stand on God's word; speak it over your life. It is powerful, alive, and transformative.

(James 4:7) *"Therefore submit to God. Resist the devil and he will flee from you."*

2. **Wait Right!** – In action and attitude. Release control, trust God and surrender to the process. Work in excellence preparing your environment (work and home) for the opportunity that will come; be ready to seize it and walk through the open door at God's appointed time!

3. **Breathe Deeply** – Taking deep breaths help you to center yourself, stop the anxiety, and tap into your inner power to think and speak more clearly. The basics of everything you need to know are already within you waiting to be brought forth.

✓ Breathe in (inhale) clarity, peace, and confidence

✓ Breathe out (exhale) negative thoughts, stress, and fear

✓ Be still and breathe your way through the process, it will calm and ground you

This was my experience and sharing of how to be prepared for the unexpected.

In closing, remember to stay positive, be encouraged and fearless. Believe what God says about you and wait expectantly with enthusiasm for the amazing things that God promises and wants to do in the lives of those who love Him and are obedient to His call.

God has a plan and purpose for your life, plans to prosper you and give you hope and a future. Work towards your life's purpose as He leads and guides. Remember that God is faithful! All you have to do is show up – available and willing; God will do the work in, through and as you.

HOW TO GET IT DONE IN EASE
AND ELEGANCE

When it comes to getting things done, internal and external resistance will readily present distractions to circumvent your best intentions. For instance, "I don't feel like it" or a tendency to put off for tomorrow what can be done today are common examples of internal resistance. External resistance can present itself through a phone call or visitor that you would rather entertain than complete the items on your list.

On the other hand, the following practices and principles can combat those distractions and assist you in getting things done in ease and elegance:

1. **Set an intention** to get the maximum results with the least amount of effort. Even if you don't know how, just intend it to be so. It may not happen overnight, but your determination and declaration of intent will eventually manifest.

2. **Make a list** of the things you feel need to be done, then spend some quiet time in prayer and meditation asking God what it is that He would have you do. Allow Spirit to guide you in prioritizing from His list. Aligning yourself with God's

agenda will streamline your goals and empower you to be more effective, productive, and motivated.

3. **Practice the Kaizen principle** of making little changes on a regular basis, like removing at least one item daily until the job is done. A perfect solution for prime procrastinating projects like clearing clutter or unpacking. Consider them as works in progress.

4. **Recruit an accountability partner** to share your set goals and to check-in with you on a weekly basis. Discuss what has been completed, set new goals, and encourage each other through the process. Having supportive help helps!

5. **Be gentle with yourself** when some things you've committed to do are not done in your desired time frame. Sometimes the lists may overlap into the next day, week, or month. Don't be discouraged or give up. It's okay to make slow steady progress toward accomplishing what you set out to do.

6. **Be grateful** for what you have accomplished no matter how small a task it may seem. Remember that any progress moves you closer from where you are to where you want to be in the process of getting things done.

Whatever challenges come while getting things done, press forward one day at a time with the belief and determination that you will succeed in completing your goals, one task at a time, in ease and elegance, as God directs your steps.

HOW TO EXPERIENCE A LIFE OF JOY EVERYDAY

Experience a joy-filled life of inner peace by practicing the following five key elements on a daily basis:

1. **BREATHE DEEPLY**

• <u>Breath is life</u> – Breathing exercises are used to manage stress, asthma, anger, and to attain various states of consciousness.

• <u>Breathing technique</u> – Deeply inhale and exhale four (4) times to a slow four (4) count of each.

> ✓ Inhale through nose, bringing breath up through chest and shoulders as stomach expands

> ✓ Exhale, releasing final breath with a "ha" sound, dropping shoulders as stomach deflates

2. **TURN WITHIN**

• <u>Meditate</u> – A moment of quiet stillness can ground you in God and prepare you to face each day victoriously. Be still and know…. If necessary, repeat a word, phrase, or chant sound to quiet the mind (i.e. peace, peace be still, or om). Sit quietly in God's presence and feel His unconditional love.

• <u>Pray</u> – Talk to God and surrender your concerns. **P**ray **U**ntil **S**omething **H**appens (PUSH). Ask Spirit a question and wait for the answer; reflect on the truth of who God is and who you are in Him; affirm yourself.

3. STIMULATE JOY

• <u>Identify</u> – the things you are passionate about and enjoy doing, then choose to use them as a tool to help you shift out of depression and negative self-talk as needed.

• <u>Determine</u> – your gifts, using the Spiritual Gifts Test, which lists, defines and provides supporting scriptures. (http://www.kodachrome.org/spiritgift).

4. BE LOVE

• <u>Love God, Yourself, and Others</u> – Use God's love as a measure to love yourself and others as He loves you.

• <u>BE the LOVE you seek</u> – Whatever you desire to experience in love from another, be that first and NOW in all your relationships. Walk in love as your way of life and you will attract the love that you are.

5. FORGIVE ALL

• <u>Forgive to be forgiven</u> – Forgiveness is a divine mandate that is required to maintain a right relationship with God and yourself.

• <u>Affirmation</u> – Unblock your flow by affirming: "All that has offended me, I forgive. Within and without, I forgive. Things past, things present, things future, I forgive. I forgive everything and everybody who can possibly need forgiveness in my past and present. I forgive positively everyone. I am free, and all others are free too. All things are cleared up between us, now and forever." ~ Catherine Ponder

• <u>Healing Mantra</u> – Ho'oponopono is an ancient Hawaiian healing mantra that means to make right. Apply it to yourself and all perceived offenders by repeating the following phrase until it resonates within you and takes the heat off your negative feelings toward another:

"I LOVE YOU * I'M SORRY *
PLEASE FORGIVE ME * THANK YOU."

You demonstrate a choice to experience joy and transform your relationships when you breathe and connect to your inner power, stimulate your joy, be the love you seek, and walk in forgiveness on a daily basis.

HOW TO BE SINGLE, SATISFIED
AND SUCCESSFUL

Defining terms for "Single" include: not married; and a separate individual person. Although singleness is the natural beginning state of human evolution, it is oftentimes not easily managed emotionally for some individuals during their young adult to middle-aged years of development. This is especially true for women who feel incomplete and unhappy with their single status, choosing to compromise their boundaries or settle for relationships that do not honor them or meet their heartfelt desires. However, there are ways to be single, satisfied and successful when viewed with the right attitude and perspective.

SINGLE – You are a spiritual being having a human experience and was birthed into this world through a divine process that requires you to develop and mature in a single state (unless you're a twin) from the womb until the dating stage of being coupled. Being single provides an opportunity to discover who you are and would like to become. Use the time to intimately know God and yourself.

Singleness does not equal loneliness. You are always

connected to the Creator, who intends for His creation to be interdependent on one another, in love.

SATISFIED – Until you are totally satisfied in your relationship with God first, and complete in yourself as a person, you are not ready for a relationship with a prospective mate. God will not take second place and is the only true source of the love you desire to experience. Love begins with God and evolves into self-love before you are able to love another as God intended.

Spend time developing your individuality and learn to enjoy your own company. Engage in activities of interest and create healthy relationships that uplift, strengthen character, and are fun. Being content in your single state will prepare you for companionship and attract the relationship you desire to experience out of love, instead of need.

SUCCESSFUL – Success is relative to your experience based on your true desire and that which generates joy in the process of living. Success is also independent of what others think or feel success is. No one can define success for you.

When you can be your authentic self, make choices in alignment to God's will and your goals, and live life on purpose doing what you love unapologetically, then you are successful.

STEPS TO SUCCESS:

1) Discover what makes you happy

2) Write it down and affirm it verbally

3) Be specific about what you like to do, how you want your life to look, what it feels like living it, and the actions you must take to make it a reality

4) Go to bed and wake up in that high vibration of feel good emotions

5) Create a mind movie to replay daily, as often as needed

You can be single, satisfied, and successful when you make time to discover who you are and develop a personal relationship with God; become complete within yourself and totally satisfied in your relationship with God; and be true to yourself, living a life that makes you feel good while doing what you enjoy.

THE FIREWALK: MY PATH TO PERSONAL FREEDOM

Introduction to the Firewalk Possibility

Firewalking is the act of walking barefoot over a bed of hot embers or stones. Walking on fire has existed for a few thousand years with records dating back to 1200 B.C.; it has a long history in many cultures as a test or proof of faith; and it has been practiced for spiritual, emotional, and physical healing. Firewalking is about squarely facing your fears and giving up belief patterns that have held you in a reality too small for your spirit. This process toward collective empowerment and healing was introduced to me at St Paul Community Baptist Church in 1997 by Jeffrey Vincent Noble (a pranic healer, motivational speaker, relationship counselor, and success coach).

The Preparation

While the men set up outside, heating the coals and roping off the path, Jeff prepared us inside by working to raise our energy level to equal or exceed that of the fire. Only then would we be able to walk safely on the fiery path. Jeff explained the firewalk ritual and shared his firewalk experience with us. When he initially asked how many of us were planning to try it, I can assure you that many a hand did not go up, including mine.

During the preparation, we were guided through some meditation exercises, visualizing our trials, traumas, and victory. We were told to determine what our place of victory would look and feel like, and then to select a representative color that we could recall later in challenging times. Finally, we role-played walking through the firewalk ritual in the sanctuary. All in all, it was like a spiritual pep rally that proved to be effective because when Jeff asked again, "How many of you are planning to walk?" several more hands went up. Mine however, was still not included. In fact, I did not do the firewalk on that first night.

Frozen In Fear

Two nights later, on Saturday, September 27, 1997 when I felt the Holy Spirit leading me, my hand went up to do the second walk. After the firewalk preparation, firewalkers were lined up in a single file while non-participants gathered along the outside of the ropes to cheer us on. The high energy saturated the air and was maintained by the intensity of the drummers' hard rhythmic beats and the people chanting, "Freeedoooom, Yes Lord Yes!" As the second person in line, I felt the need for some extra power so while everyone else was chanting, I was mentally reciting scriptures. *"I can do all things through Christ who strengthens me."* (Philippians 4:13); *"I look to the hills from whence cometh my help."* (Psalms 121:1);); *"God is my refuge and strength, a present help in trouble."* (Psalm 46:1); *God has not given me the spirit of fear."* (2 Timothy 1:7).

As I approached the fiery coal-lined path, I stepped on some hot embers that had fallen undetected from the shovel into the grass. All scripture recitation immediately fled my mind, replaced by this resounding paralyzing thought, "*OH NO! IF I CAN FEEL THIS, WHAT'S GOING TO HAPPEN WHEN I STEP ONTO THAT 15 FOOT, 1200 DEGREE BED OF HOT COALS!*" I dragged my foot against the grass in an unsuccessful attempt to scrape off the clinging embers as my steps faltered into position at the head of the coals.

Physically frozen in fear, I heard a quiet reassuring voice filtering through the loud drumming and chanting, streaming through my left ear: "This is the moment you've been preparing for ... think about all the things you want to overcome in your life ... you can do it!" Sensing my hesitation, Jeff had instantly stepped into action with motivating words of encouragement. My thoughts raced, *I can't stay where I am because I'm holding up a long line of firewalkers; I can't turn back and let fear defeat me now and haunt me later at the crossroads of future challenges; if I don't cross at this moment, I probably never will; HELP Lord!*

Liberating Victory!

> "*Behold, I give you the authority to trample on serpents and scorpions, and over all the power of the enemy, and nothing shall by any means hurt you.*" (Luke 10:19)

Suddenly, transcending peace calmed my mind and spoke to my spirit. I felt and heard the Holy Spirit say, "Even if you feel it, I will not allow you to be harmed, those are dancing feet." I pressed forward with determined steps, propelled by a new level of faith, the rhythm of the African drums, and the chanting of the saints.

I victoriously crossed over to the other side unburned and full with praise and thanksgiving to God! There were two men waiting to grab hold of each arm and spray the soles of my feet with water. But, they seemed to have missed the spot where the stinging embers took up residence. My sister-friend Cassandra A. Young (Cassie) was also waiting for me, on the other side of the hot coals, with a hug and reminder to step into my victory color and center myself. As I visualized the color purple, a series of piercing screams erupted from what felt like the depths of my toes and traveled through my body and out of my mouth. It was rooted in emotions that had long been suppressed and seeking release for over 25 years.

Although liberating for me, poor Cassie was unfortunately locked in my exuberant embrace of joyous jumps and sanctified shrieks. Where I lost an earring that night, she most likely experienced partial hearing loss. As for those hot embers that had lodged in the bottom of my foot, I was thankful because they temporarily left three indentations that served as a confirmation to the realness of the event. I had previously heard skeptic stories like, "The coals used in firewalks aren't really hot and don't burn." The dents were also a reminder of my accomplishment and for me, represented the presence of the Father, Son and Holy Spirit, safely guiding me across the coals.

Lasting Benefits

In the face of fear, God resurrected my courage and continues to motivate me with empowering peace, confirmation and scripture. Crossing those hot coals revealed my limitless potential, demonstrating "*I can do all things through Christ who strengthens me*" (Philippians 4:13). Moreover, I continue to glorify God, heal self, and edify others through gifts of encouragement, writing, praise and worship, and dance. Whether my body is feeling well or ill, I press forward knowing that "*When I am weak, then I am strong*" (2 Corinthians 12:10).

HOW I FOUGHT FEAR WITH FAITH

2008 held some highlights that were obtained strictly by pressing through fear to walk in faith. My God-orchestrated 2008 highlights included: publishing my first book, "On Solid Ground: Inspirational Poetry For All Occasions," with Author House; purchasing space to promote my book at Dr. Suzan Johnson Cook's (Dr. Sujay) Moving Up Conference at the NY Marriott Hotel; my first official book signing at Crossroads Tabernacle (CT); facilitating a "No More Drama" small group bible session at CT's annual Ladies Retreat; guest speaker on "Hurting Hearts," a Brooklyn Community Access Television (BCAT) program; guest speaker on Boost In Your Bathrobe, a daily weekday morning prayer, praise & inspiration conference call; and joining Dr. Sujay's newly formed Grace Dance Ministry and ministering through dance at the world famous Apollo Theater on three occasions during her Sunday morning services that season.

As exciting as it may sound and was, make no mistake, fear was present before and during! All was accomplished to the glory of God by standing firmly on the solid ground of His word. I accepted the opportunities because, in knowing that God had provided them and presented them to me, "How could I not." Once accepted, I had to sit in His presence and seek a word for myself and His people; get centered and draw strength to do the *next* that He was calling me to (each round goes higher and higher). In identifying and confessing what the fear was, the Holy Spirit assuaged it with the Word; and then I chose to receive it and hold God accountable to a positive outcome, trusting that He would not let me be put to shame.

(Joel 2:26) *"You shall eat in plenty and be satisfied, and praise the name of the LORD your God, who has dealt wondrously with you; and My people shall never be put to shame."*

FROM FEARFUL TO FAITH-FILLED

After living the first half of my life making decisions governed by fear, I now make faith based choices in spite of fear. God has proven to be faithful in every situation and always gives me what I need and instruction on how to proceed in order to accomplish each task. In stepping out in faith in spite of the fear, I have become more confident of my abilities in Him, learning that I truly can do all things through Christ, who strengthens me.

In preparing for the BCAT appearance, I was afraid that I wouldn't know what to say or that the answers would not flow because I didn't know what I would be asked and I felt totally outside of my comfort zone in this first-time type of speaking experience (TV! Wow God). God addressed my fears and stabilized my faith through the following word and scriptures:

God's word to me was: "Fear Not! Do it afraid. Trust Me and surrender all."

The scriptures were: (Joshua 1:9) *"Have I not commanded you? Be strong and of good courage; do not be afraid, nor be dismayed, for the LORD your God is with you wherever you go."*

(Habakkuk 2:2-3) *"Then the LORD answered me and said: "Write the vision and make it plain on tablets, that he may run who reads it. For the vision is yet for an appointed time; but at the end it will speak, and it will not lie. Though it tarries, wait for it; because it will surely come, it will not tarry."*

> *(Jeremiah 1:9) "Then the LORD put forth His hand*
> *and touched my mouth, and the LORD said to me:*
> *"Behold, I have put My words in your mouth."*

LESSON LEARNED

God was with me as promised and showed Himself through the entire process. I learned that as long as I show up in faith and obedience, humbled and surrendered, God will meet me where I am and make my way successful.

I encourage you to also: Fear not! Pursue your dreams and remember…. You are not doing it alone. God is with you to help you co-create the life you desire. He will direct your steps and make the necessary provisions for you to experience the desires of your heart.

MY FORGIVENESS JOURNEY

The ability to forgive is essential to moving forward in life and being forgiven by God. When you choose to hold onto the hurt, you only punish and imprison yourself.

In talking about my forgiveness journey, I have to begin with an unforgiving nature that reared up as a child. You see, because I was more of a loner and considered myself a very good and loyal friend to others, I had a hard and fast rule to cut off anyone, who I felt betrayed me. This applied especially to those I let inside my small inner-circle and there were no second chances given.

PRE-SALVATION CASUALTIES OF MY UNFORGIVENESS

1. **My Father** – The 1st casualty was my father. For years, I had the misunderstanding that he abandoned me and quit his job so that he wouldn't have to pay child support for my sister and me. And so, from the time I was in elementary school, I barely talked to him when I saw him and never showed him any respect or love. I emotionally disconnected and referred to him by his last name only. I maintained a cold distant front at all times, even when he inadvertently ended

up at my wedding and in some of the pictures years later.

2. **My Best Friend** – The 2nd casualty was my best friend, who grew up around the corner from me. We spent a lot of time together and used to have contests to see who could name the most synonyms, antonyms, and write the tiniest. We were "Besties" through elementary school and JHS until one day when we had a substitute band teacher and decided to cut class for the first time. She got caught and ratted out the rest of us. That was it for me, we never hung out after that and even though we went to the same HS, we never really reconciled until her mom took ill years later.

POST SALVATION CASUALTY OF UNFORGIVENESS

1. **Church Sister-friend** – She was an aspiring hair stylist, who I supported as her hair model from beauty school through hair salon job interviews. One day she was having an event at the church and had asked me to participate, so I put off having my hair done until that day. Long story short, the day got long and she decided not to do my hair, which was a mess and I was traveling on public transportation immediately following the event. I felt totally disregarded and taken for granted. I instituted and maintained an intentional distance for quite some time afterward.

FORGIVENESS AWARENESS

1. **Church Sister** – My first awareness of being out of order started with my church sister situation. I felt strongly convicted about my attitude as if God were saying, "How dare you not forgive someone when I forgave you!" I realized that it was not an option, but a requirement to forgive in order to stay in right relationship with God and continue to receive forgiveness for myself.
(Matthew 6: 14-15) "*For if you forgive other people when they sin*

against you, your heavenly Father will also forgive you. But if you do not forgive others their sins, your Father will not forgive your sins."

2. **Spiritual Development Class** – In 2007, one of my spiritual development classes dealt with a term called "withholding" and I realized that I had done that with my dad. I learned that when I withhold myself from others, I am basically withholding from myself because you can't shut yourself down from others without blocking your good and shutting yourself off from a mutual exchange of love and God opportunities.

CONSEQUENCES/LOSSES

1. **Best Friend** – With my childhood friend, I lost out on a best friend relationship that challenged me. We were like iron sharpening iron in our early years and she also belonged to a church. My first time in church was in college when it could have been during my childhood had I not distanced myself. I could only imagine how I might have developed differently had we stayed friends. She became a lawyer and waited to marry when she was ready and felt it was the right relationship. Relationships were an emotional area of struggle and inner-turmoil for many years in my life.

2. **Church Sister** – With my Church-Sister, during my distancing from her, she made a poor and regrettable choice that she might not have made had I been available to talk her through it. I felt bad about it for a long time when she told me. I repented and was convicted in the fact that I had no right to hold anything over anyone; and am very grateful to God for His grace, mercy and forgiving nature toward us all.

3. **Dad** – With my Dad, I lost out on getting to know him and sharing God with him when his life took a turn for the worst. I experienced guilt and fear for his soul because although I had become civil with him after salvation, I was

still emotionally distant and never showed any love for him or toward him. My forgiveness of him unfortunately came after his death.

FORGIVENESS TOOLS/RITUALS

1. **My Dad Forgiveness Process**:

   • Memorial Service for deceased fathers – Wrote 2 letters of forgiveness, 1 asking him for forgiveness and 1 forgiving him; and then placed them in a coffin set up for the symbolic ceremony.

   • Wrote a "Posthumous Love" poem about my forgiveness process with him:

POSTHUMOUS LOVE

It was long after his death
when I gave birth to this love.

For most of his life,
I was distant and cold.
I only spoke in a manner
that was contemptuous and bold.

I'm not proud, I'm just stating the facts.

We often hear,
"Beware the wrath of a woman scorned";
But the consequences of a brother spurned
can be just as painful, generative, and wrong.

Selfish, irresponsible, and uncaring;
to me, that is where he stood.
I was just too young to remember
the heydays of his fatherhood.
Blinded by partial knowledge

and the stagnant perception of a child;
A hardened heart that would not let me see
the best of him...also present inside of me.

My journey to this posthumous love
began when I got saved.
Forgive to be forgiven was how
this reconciliation road was to be paved.

I grew to speak with a civil tongue
and intentionally quench the negative thoughts;
But, the desire to demonstrate any love
seemed to be forever lost.

I don't remember ever calling him "daddy"
or saying, "I love you" to his face.
But, I finally got the opportunity to reconcile
thanks to the ministry of Pastor Youngblood
and God's saving grace.

I learned to search out the good and
make peace with his spirit, and be at peace within myself.
I learned that harboring ill-feelings was self-destructive
and that Love is the key above all else.

I discovered his enriching legacy
transmitted to my sister Renee and me,
his good heart, his sense of humor,
and his dancing ability.

And the one thing that I hold dearest,
my childhood desire, the greatest gift
is my younger brother William;
dad's namesake and physical image,
who I met when I was 36.

To conceive this posthumous love I now experience

for my earthly father, who gave me life;
I opened my heart and took the steps to grow
in the healing power of the resurrected Christ.

(1 Corinthians 13:12) "*For now we see through a glass, darkly; but then face to face: now I know in part; but then shall I know even as also I am known.*"

• Spiritually Journaling assignment – The Dialogue method by Richard Peace allowed me to address my dad issues, where guilt, pain and questions emerged. The steps include:

✓ Recall and write out in great detail the whole situation

✓ Offer the situation to God in prayer

✓ Begin the dialogue regarding the details

(This experience and result is documented in Vol. 1, "How To Uncover, Heal & Release Painful Life Experiences").

2. **Ho'oponopono** – I use this technique as needed when I am annoyed or angry with folks. You think of the person or memory and say audible or silently, "I love you, I'm sorry, Please forgive me, Thank you." This method is discussed in Joe Vitale's book, Zero Limits.

I learned the mantra from Rev. Valerie Love and was taught to include, "I forgive all." I repeat the mantra whenever I feel negative energy about the people I am forgiving or the stories I attached to them. It is a tool for unconditional love, radical forgiveness and gratitude.

3. **Forgiveness Diet** – Ask Spirit to bring to mind all people and or situations you need to forgive including yourself, and do the following exercise for seven consecutive days:

- Before Noon, write 35 times: "I, (your name), forgive (name of person) totally and unconditionally." (If more than one name comes up just list them all in one sentence, **do not** write the statement 35 times for each person individually).

- Before Midnight, write 35 times: "I, (your name), forgive myself totally and unconditionally. I am free to move on to wholeness and completion."

You may be surprised to see who comes to mind. People came up that I thought were forgiven. I found that there are levels of healing and learning.

> **NOTE**: If you miss a day or time, you must start the consecutive seven-day cycle over. This technique is an abridged version based on Iyanla Vanzant's sharing in Tapping The Power Within.

4. **A Prayer of Forgiveness & Release** – I wrote the following prayer for a retreat event and now share it with you for use in your forgiveness-healing journey:

Beloved Almighty Healer
and Sovereign Creator of the Universe;
Let your will, as it is in heaven,
be done in all the earth.

To the Son, Lord Jesus,
the Anointed One
and Ruler of my heart;
In you, I am forgiven and
have received a prosperous new start.

Precious Holy Spirit,
my Comforter and Peace;
Thank you for continual revelations
of all the negative and hindering things I must release.

I surrender my life totally–
Heart, mind, body and soul;
Search me, purge me, and cleanse me
of past issues I have yet to let go.

I confess all erroneous thinking,
poor choices and actions not aligned with You,
which resulted in unpleasant consequences
that were challenging to survive through.

I now release the pain, hurt, trauma
and disappointment in my life,
forgiving self, first, and then all others
I perceived as contributors to my experiences of strife.

I petition You, Lord, with this heartfelt prayer
of forgiveness and release,
and trust that the healing and wholeness
begun in me will be made complete.

For past, present, and future
Healing on deeper levels,
I thank you in Jesus name.
And So It Is! Amen.

LESSON: People are not mind readers and will do what you let them. You have to teach people how to treat you and tell them when they hurt your feelings or offend you with their words or actions. Communicate before you separate. You still may need to distance yourself in the end OR you just may reap the fruits of a salvaged worthy life-long close relationship.

(Matthew 18:15) *"If your brother or sister in God's family does something wrong, go and tell them what they did wrong. Do this when you are alone with them. If they listen to you, then you have helped them to be your brother or sister again.*

LEARNING THE LESSONS OF LIFE

PASS OR REPEAT

Learn the lesson or repeat the class. If you do not learn the lessons in your life, you will not pass the test. You might get a little further along than you were before, maybe even get more answers right the next time around, but you will ultimately still fail the test if you haven't learned the lesson well. Learning the lesson requires the ability to understand it within the core of your being, knowing how and why it applies to you and your life situations. Some people may learn the lesson the hard way, while others learn the lesson the easy way.

As you read the following learned lesson from my own life, reflect on your own situations and assess your learning process. Are you learning the lessons in your life or do you find yourself failing tests and repeating classes?

It took me 22 years to learn some key lessons that took root and bloomed only after surviving a divorce, two disabling car accidents, and three bouts with disabling respiratory ailments, all clearly illustrating that I used to learn my lessons the hard way. Unfortunately or fortunately, depending on whose perspective, I was one of those individuals who had to personally experience some things to fully understand them. Some mistakes I've had to make on my own instead of learning from what I was told or observed others do. I needed to experience the whys of the situation in order to grasp it in a way that would be lasting and transforming.

To all inexperienced learners of hard lessons, be advised that this form of learning has proven to be most painful, more often than not. However, there is a comforting, encouraging, and reassuring upside, which is that:

> If you sincerely want to learn the lessons for your life,
> God will work with you, in and through you, lovingly
> (yet firmly) and patiently until you learn the lesson
> and victoriously pass the test!

A TEST

During a 7-week medical leave from work in 2006, I underwent a spiritual and physical reconstruction; nearly lost out on a prepaid nonrefundable Caribbean vacation; and stressed over educational plans for that year. The 7-week medical leave covered a 9 week period because I had miserably failed the test that was presented after the first four weeks when I had returned to work for two weeks, resulting in me repeating the class for another three weeks. Although I knew the right answers the first time around, I overanalyzed my situation, wrestled with my spirit, and made the wrong choices. This experience can be broken down as follows:

Test Topic: Your Body, God's Temple

Lesson Learned: Do not focus on physical symptoms, the possible interruption of future plans or give negative thoughts a foothold in your mind. Instead, fix your eyes on Jesus only, be Spirit-led and obedient in taking care of your body, whatever the surrounding circumstances.

Scripture References:

(Matthew 6:34) *"Therefore do not worry about tomorrow, for tomorrow will worry about its own things. Sufficient for the day is its own trouble."*

(Proverbs 16:9) *"A man's heart plans his way, but the Lord directs his steps."*

(James 4:13-15) *"Come now, you say, "Today or tomorrow we will go to such and such a city, spend a year there, buy and sell, and make a profit"; whereas you do not know what will happen tomorrow…. Instead you ought to say, "If the Lord wills, we shall live and do this or that."*

The Lord reiterated some truths that I had previously experienced and held on an intellectual level, but this time He inscribed those truths on the walls of my heart. Am I certain that I will make all the right choices on future test? No, nor am I worried about passing the next one. I am and will continue to be a work in process on this side of heaven, test by test, one day at a time, walking in a state of repentance, striving to be more like Jesus until the good work that has begun in me is complete. Through it all, I've learned that some battles belong to God alone; I need not fear, flee or fight, just stand in position, be still, give praise, and see the salvation of the Lord.

SHARE YOUR LESSONS

So what is your story? What lessons are you learning? Are you learning them the easy way or the hard way?

As long as you live, you can be assured that you will experience life challenges. Always know that there is a lesson to be learned in each and every one; it is not what we encounter in life, but how we respond to and handle the situations that come our way. Instead of reacting in fear and uncertainty, look to God and use the experience as an opportunity to grow stronger and wiser through your journey.

(John 16:33) *"In the world you will have tribulation, but be of good cheer, I have overcome the world."*

PRAISE REPORT RESULTS OF A PRAYER AND FASTING CONSECRATION

I experienced God in new and amazing ways during a 21-day consecration with my church, Apostolic Temple of Jesus Christ. The consecration included one meal per day and prayer services on Mondays, Wednesdays and Fridays at 6 a.m. and 7 p.m. from Monday, Jan. 7 – Sunday, Jan. 27, 2013. The focus was to draw closer to God and not ask for anything, but seek Him first and trust that He would add all other things. As I focused on being about God's business, He provided for my present needs and answered some desires of my heart. I share my prayer and fasting praise report results with you to encourage you on your journey with our faithful God.

CONSECRATION RESULTS

Week One

God showed His mindfulness of me from day one and I felt His love intimately.

• **Transportation** – On the first day of consecration, I

desired to attend the 6 a.m. prayer service. However, when the alarm went off at 5 a.m. I felt my body required more rest because I didn't go to sleep till 3 a.m. At 5:30 a.m., I had a mind to go, but wasn't feeling the cold and darkness outside because I usually walk to church. At 5:52 a.m., Spirit prompted me to go so I got up and dressed, trusting God. I left the house at 6:20 a.m., walked around the corner and was offered a ride from a childhood friend on his way to work. After service, I got a ride with the Deacon who lives near me and an open invitation to ride to and fro whenever needed. By week 3, I had two other members extending transportation assistance for other church services as well. *God watches over me!*

• **Support** – My mom was 100% on board with my fast, ensuring that my one meal was full and satisfying throughout the 21-days. *Good looking out Mom!*

• **Writing** – Wrote an article on Prayer and Fasting to post in my NY Christian Living examiner.com column and a poem about my church to post in my hubpages.com portfolio. Thank God for a combined 200+ writings currently shared on both platforms!

• **Potential Client** – A potential self-publishing book client that I met when I spoke at a writing event in November requested a follow-up consultation and set a "ready" target date for March 25, 2013. And she shared some information that resonated with me regarding One Billion Rising, a V-Day event annually held on February 14, to end violence against women. (**Update**: She never followed through on the publishing, but I participated in the One Billing Rising Campaign in major ways that supported my healing on deeper levels and the healing of others).

• **Leadership** – Stepped up to the divine opportunity to lead "Women of Praise" dance ministry in prayer, warm-up and rehearsal until dance coordinator arrived from her meeting. *Where God leads me, I will follow.*

• **Divine Encouragement** – Sunday was an emotional day because some things that were said disturbed my spirit before service started; but during the call to worship while at the altar praying, one of my church sisters came over and embraced me. I relaxed into the hug and wept. She told me that God said, "Don't worry." She also told me to ask her if I was in need of anything. Another member also blessed me with a gift item. *God is my comfort!*

Week Two

God was my provision, allowing me to "BE" more and "DO" less.

• **Financial provision** – A former love, wonderful friend, and good client deposited money in my business account just because. Next day, a prayer line sister sent me a donation for my inspirational contributions Mondays – Fridays. Thus, I was able to focus on my consecration and not be anxious about making money. *God is the Source of my unlimited supply.*

• **Family** – My father's son, the brother I always wanted and love dearly, posted a Facebook comment saying he loved me and would keep in touch. *Thank you, God!*

• **Spiritual Elevation** – First Lady asked me to be one of the speakers at her Women's Day program in April. *My gifts make room for me.*

• **Favor** – My moon cycle came a week early instead of during the full week of service when I had to be on my feet and out about town. *God works all things together for my good.*

• **Divine Encouragement** – Received a God message

during the Sunday service benediction when I felt an urgent need to hear and experience Him in a mighty way. The minister said that a shifting was taking place- first a shaking up, then a shift, after which everything would begin to harmonize and fall into place. Later that evening, I participated on a teleseminar about the "invoking" prayer technique that shifted and ignited my prayer experience. *God rewards diligent seekers.*

Week Three

God met me where I was and empowered me to be of service through a busy and emotional week.

• **God shift** – Because of my prior evening pranic healing commitments in Brooklyn, I was unable to attend the 7 p.m. prayer services; therefore, I intended to make the 6 a.m. services. However, my sleeping patterns had been extremely out of order with me going to sleep anywhere from 3 – 6 a.m. So on Sunday night, I told my mind, spirit, and body that they could be up till 6 a.m. if they wanted to, but "we" would be in church come morning whether "we" were just getting up or still up. I went to bed at a better hour and woke up alert, rested, and ready to start my day. Also my prayers, encouragement, and acts of service have been passionately bolder and more confident. *I speak things into existence.*

• **Ministry** – I served through prayer and healing, during the healing night for Pranic healers; Helped with the editing of a friend's book that was about to be published; Shared the message about Prayer and Fasting on the prayer line; Gave remarks at the home-going service, wrote two articles and created a photo album in memory and celebration of widely loved college mate, Kelvin Hicks. *I can do all things through Christ who strengthens me.*

• **Divine overflow** – A prayer line sister referred a

potential self-publishing book client, who contacted me; A church sister asked if I would share one of my poems at the Pastor's Aide "Night of Praise" service in March; My articles' earnings increased close to monthly payout threshold; Closing consecration service was high powered and liberating with praise and the "If these walls could talk" sermon; Another church sister gifted me with some new clothes that included an outfit that I needed to serve communion in for the following Sunday. *My God supplies all my needs.*

(Matthew 17:20-21) "He said to them, Because of the littleness of your faith [that is, your lack of [firmly relying trust]. For truly I say to you, if you have faith that is living] like a grain of mustard seed, you can say to this mountain, Move from here to yonder place, and it will move; and nothing will be impossible to you.

²¹ "But this kind does not go out except by prayer and fasting."

I RISE FOR THE VOICELESS, VALUELESS AND VICTIMIZED

The Catalyst

February 2013 was an interesting month of healing and liberation for me through the worldwide campaign "**One Billion Rising**." The **V-Day** organization initiated this global call of solidarity to raise awareness, educate, and protect women, heal the past and stop the present and future violence against women and young girls because statistics indicate that 1 in every 3 women will be raped or beaten in their lifetime. Those stats affect one billion women on the planet.

"One Billion Rising" resonated with me because I was one of those statistics, who had been raped on two separate occasions during my college years. I share my story, the lessons learned, and the beautiful awareness and purpose that arose from the ashes for anyone who has ever felt voiceless, undervalued or victimized. It is for you that I have been called and purposed to rise and speak.

Before I learned to speak out; value myself as much as others; and live victoriously, I experienced many victimizing situations that I silently internalized to my detriment.

Lessons Of The First Encounter

The **first rape** happened when I was a 17 year old naïve College freshman. I had gotten nauseously drunk at a neighboring college dorm party and was carried back to my dorm facility in a barely conscious state. I remember the actual violation as a fictional dream: *The perpetrator kept pushing up on me at the party after everyone had left, and all I could and wanted to do was lay on the wooden wall-bench and sleep.*

I woke up the next morning in my bed feeling a great deal of discomfort in my vaginal area. Upon asking my roommate if something happened, her boyfriend excused himself, and she proceeded to tell me that a known friend of her boyfriend had his way with me (after they had let him into the room). It was the first time I had ever been sexually penetrated.

I swallowed the anger that turned to hate, never spoke a word about it to her, him, the school administration or the police. I stewed in shame and silence, even when my roommate used to allow him in the room to watch TV. It was my first and only experience with hate for an individual; it was intense and self-destructive, keeping me in bondage and eating me from the inside out. I used to feel like my head would explode from the suppressed anger whenever he was in my space. I learned to release it through the daily devotional readings from Guideposts and soul cries to a God I didn't know personally at the time. It took me 20 years to process the pain of the experience and release it through the tears of acknowledgement and sound.

1. **My first step toward healing** was to acknowledge my lack of responsibility in contributing to the outcome of that evening. I mixed my drinks, drank too much and didn't know my limit, which left me vulnerable and in a position to be taken advantage of and victimized.

2. **My second step toward healing** was in the spiritual awakening. The dynamics of the experience expedited my path toward God because it created trust issues that caused me to cry out to God to have my back, so that I didn't have to exist in a world looking over my shoulder worrying about who was going to do me dirty. I couldn't imagine living that way and God heard me. I became more aware of His nudges and messages through people handing out tracks, a friend taking me to church for the first time, and the Daily Guideposts devotional readings. A few years later, I joined the College Christian Club, the dorm bible study group, and I started attending church regularly.

Acknowledgements Of The Second Time

In 1981, I joined the church, accepted Jesus Christ as my Lord and Savior, got baptized and strove to live a holy life. And then, it happened again. Even though I was sober and living in obedience to the word of God, He allowed me to be violated by a student I used to be involved with on an intimate level before salvation. He stopped by the dorm to visit me and I thought nothing of it because we had mutually decided to end the relationship and parted as friends. It was summertime and the dorm was basically empty. I worked for the school over the summer cleaning out dorm apartments to prepare them for the following semester. When he started making moves, I tried to explain that I wasn't interested and that I was saved and celibate, but he became very aggressive.

I begged and pleaded through tears for him to not do this thing and for God to stop it, but he was in a selfish sexual frenzy and overpowered me. My mind and body went numb because I could not comprehend how God could let this happen to me when I was trying to live right with my whole heart. When he was done, he went out the door and I went to the bathroom and tried to scrub myself clean in the shower as the water and tears flowed. It reminded me of a movie scene where the victim tries to scrub herself raw, removing the touch, smell, memories … and also for me, the spiritual doubt that was trying to rise up and take root.

1. **My first healing thought** at making any sense of this experience was that before I knew God personally, I had an intuitive knowing that the things I experienced as a teenager and young adult were not just for my growth and development. I was going through for others and I saw visions of me speaking to other youth and young women about the issues of life. This experience emphasized and confirmed that knowing because, "How could I inspire others through their challenges if I've never experienced any of my own?"

2. **My second and most profound awareness** is that God is all there is and He is my reason for being. Outside of Him, I am nothing and would cease to survive, thrive, or live. No matter what I experience in this life, I will not allow it to come between me and my God because I am fully persuaded that He works all things together for my good; and what man means for evil, He will use for a greater good to benefit the world at large. It was true in this instance and again when my 15-year old great-niece was stabbed in the heart and died in the street. I felt the deepest pain to date. I cried, I breathed, and then I allowed God's grace to be sufficient and His joy to be my strength. Then and now, I continue to praise Him and press forward in the things of God.

To the **VOICELESS**, I encourage you to pray for opportunities to speak up and tell your truth out loud, and then do it. Use the opportunity to do so within spiritual communities like The Love Journey, Inc. inspirational conference call, whether with comments to the messages, or love shout outs during the after call:

✓ Prepare yourself by setting the intention to speak daily

✓ Listen to the message

✓ Take notes as to what resonates with you and why

✓ Share at the appointed time

You have a story to tell. You telling it liberates others and gives them the power and permission to do the same.

To the **UNDERVALUED**, I encourage you to learn who you are in God and believe it. You are fearfully and wonderfully made, a royal priesthood chosen by God with your picture tattooed on the palms of His hands. It is critical and biblically sound guidance for you to first love God, who is LOVE, and then learn to love and value yourself before you can love anybody else or attract the love you desire to experience.

✓ Read God's word to learn who He is and His great love for you

✓ Expose yourself to the teachings and apply what you learn

✓ Receive the love, believe the love, and BE the love

To the **VICTIMIZED**, I encourage you to believe that no weapon formed against you shall prosper because you are more than a conqueror and nothing can separate you from God's love. In God, your name is victory! You possess the divine power and authority to have dominion over the earth, to speak things into existence and bind and loose things on earth that God will bind and loose in heaven. His word says it; I believe it and that settles it! Check it out for yourself and **appropriate God's sharp and living word** in your life.

I pressed forward and graduated college successfully, in spite of the trials and traumas I experienced. Glory be to God!

JOANNE MEEKINS
COMMUNITY
MENTAL HEALTH

Dean's List '81, MLK Scholarship, Booster Squad: Co-Captain '78-'79, Sweetheart-Iota Phi Theta, Dorm Desk Manager, Peer Counselor, Christian Fellowship

I thank God that through the **One Billion Rising campaign**, I have been able to fully release those events of the past and heal on a deeper level in global support, awareness, education, and protection for women and **young girls**.

I RISE for the Voiceless, the Undervalued,
and the Victimized.

I RISE FOR YOU!

ABOUT THE AUTHOR

Christian Writer Jo Anne Meekins is the owner of Inspired 4 U Ministries, LLC and Inspired 4 U Publications. She is also a Faith-Based Speaker, Publisher, Self-Publishing Book Coach, and Author of the recently released 3-volume series "Living a Vocal, Valued and Victorious Life," which includes:

1. How To Uncover, Heal & Release Painful Life Experiences
2. How To Press Forward & Shift To A Higher Level
3. How To Know God Better & Love Yourself More

Additional biblically-based books are:

4. How To Self-Publish in Excellence within 10-Days: A step-by-step guide to self-publishing via CreateSpace
5. For Such A Time As This
6. On Solid Ground: Inspirational Poetry For All Occasions

Her mission is to inspire customers and clients to live life passionately, on purpose, and in excellence through her inspirational products, information and services. She empowers women to speak their truth out loud, value themselves, and BE victorious over unfavorable circumstances and situations. Likewise, she assists writers in publishing their projects in a polished and professional manner.

Native New Yorker Jo Anne Meekins is a graduate of New York Institute of Technology with a Bachelor of Science in Community Mental Health. She also has Certificates in Poetry and Journalism from Writers Institute; and

Communication Skills from NYU School of Continuing and Professional Studies. Her work experience includes 7-years as a Policy & Procedure Writer for Healthfirst, Inc. where she wrote training manuals, desk aids, and policies and procedures.

Contact Jo Anne for more information, bookings or services at:

- Email:JoAnneMeekins@inspired4uministries.com
- Web: http://inspired4uministries.com

www.ingramcontent.com/pod-product-compliance
Lightning Source LLC
Chambersburg PA
CBHW071428040426
42445CB00012BA/1304